TRACKING ANIMALS

A CHAPTER BOOK

BY KIRSTEN HALL

children's press®
A Division of Scholastic Inc.
New York   Toronto   London   Auckland   Sydney
Mexico City   New Delhi   Hong Kong
Danbury, Connecticut

This book is dedicated to the scientists it features—
who are interested not only in looking *for* amazing
animals, but also in looking *after* them.

ACKNOWLEDGMENTS

The author would like to thank the following people for their time and help in
making this book happen: Katy Payne, Principle Investigator, The Elephant Listening
Project; Melissa Groo, Research Assistant, The Elephant Listening Project;
Patricia Morris, Assistant Manager, UC Natural Reserve, Año Nuevo;
Kathryn A. Zagzebski, Stranding Manager, The Marine Mammal Center;
Dr. P. J. DeVries, Director, Center for Biodiversity Studies, Milwaukee Public
Museum; Dr. Tracey K. Brown, Assistant Professor, Department of Biological
Sciences, California State University, San Marcos.

Library of Congress Cataloging-in-Publication Data

Hall, Kirsten.
  Tracking animals : a chapter book / by Kirsten Hall.
    p. cm. — (True tales)
  Includes bibliographical references and index.
  ISBN 0-516-25186-4 (lib. bdg.)   0-516-25459-6 (pbk.)
  1. Animal behavior—Juvenile literature. 2. Tracking and trailing—Juvenile literature.
I. Title. II. Series.
  QL751.5.H25 2005
  591.5—dc22
                                    2004028459

1 2 3 4 5 6 7 8 9 10 R 14 13 12 11 10 09 08 07 06 05

CONTENTS

INTRODUCTION

Have you ever wondered what animals do when we're not looking? What do they say to one another? Where do they hide? Meet four scientists who track animals, or follow their trails, in order to find out.

Katy Payne uses special recorders to tape the sounds made by elephants. By listening to the tapes, she discovered that elephants speak a secret language. Patricia Morris rescued an orphaned sea lion pup. When the sea lion was ready, it was released into the wild. Thanks to high-tech tracking devices, Patricia knows that it survived. For three months, Phil DeVries traveled the world in search of insects. He made a **documentary** about what he found during his travels. In San Diego, reptiles are losing their homes to people. Tracey Brown is studying where these reptiles live in order to save their homes.

Each of these scientists has tracked an animal and now has an incredible story to tell.

CHAPTER ONE

EAVESDROPPING ON ELEPHANTS

Katy Payne watched the elephants in their cage. She had spent many days with them at the Washington Park Zoo in Michigan City, Indiana. Now, it was time to say good-bye. She would miss their company.

On her flight home to New York, Katy thought about the elephants. She remembered feeling a sort of throbbing in the air when she was with them. The feeling reminded her of when she had sung in a choir.

Katy Payne

In the wild, elephants live in groups.

Organ pipes

Sometimes, when she had stood close to the organ's large pipes, she had sensed such a throbbing. That was when the organ's deepest note was being played. She had felt the note more strongly than she had heard it.

Katy realized that the throbbing she had felt near the elephants might have been sounds that they were making. The elephants might have been calling to one another, using sounds too low-pitched for human ears to hear.

Katy Payne is an animal researcher at Cornell University in Ithaca, New York. For many years, she studied whales with her husband. They listened to whale calls and songs and tried to understand them. Katy listened to whales for more than fifteen years before growing curious about elephants.

Katy studied the songs of humpback whales.
Only the male whales sing.

When Katy returned home, she spoke to her friend, Carl Hopkins. Carl is also a scientist at Cornell. Katy told Carl that she wanted to learn more about how elephants **communicate**. Carl agreed to lend her some of his special research equipment to record the elephant sounds.

Katy asked two co-workers to help her with the project. The research team took Carl's recording machine to the Washington Park Zoo. They used it to tape-record the elephants. The recorder was left on for days, even when it seemed that the elephants were silent.

Katy waited until she was back in Ithaca again before listening to the zoo recordings. In Carl's office, they played the tapes back ten times faster than the recording speed.

Katy listens to tapes in her office at Cornell.

Elephants use their large ears to pick up sounds.

As she and Carl listened to the tapes, they almost couldn't believe what they were hearing. The elephants had been making sounds that were below the range of human hearing. Speeding up the tapes made the range of sound higher. Now the sounds were **audible** to the human ear.

In 1999, Katy went to Africa to study elephants in the wild. There, Katy and her coworkers set up dozens of recording machines in forests. The lowest, loudest elephant calls travel miles through the forest.

Katy and her research team have learned that females use certain calls when they call to males.

The recording machines are placed high in the trees.

Katy and her team listen to the taped elephant calls.

They use other kinds of calls when they are rounding up their children. Calves use different calls to alert their mothers that they are hungry and scared.

Elephant calf

13

Wildlife rangers stack ivory tusks that they took from poachers.

Unfortunately, the lives of African elephants are in danger. **Poachers** kill elephants for their ivory tusks. Ivory is a popular carving material. It is used to make boxes, jewelry, hair combs, and pencil holders.

Katy hopes that her work will help keep elephants safe. Her goal reaches far beyond the African forests. By understanding how elephants communicate, Katy gathers important information about their behavior. One day, she hopes to use this information in ways that will protect all elephants.

Ivory decoration

CHAPTER TWO

SAVING ARTEMIS

Patricia Morris opened the doors to the crates and stepped aside. Two sea lions peered out, eyes wide. Very cautiously, one seal came out of its crate and onto a rock. The second sea lion joined the first. Slowly, they began to explore. As they made their way down toward the water, Patricia hoped that they would live long lives. They were on their own, now.

Patricia Morris

One of the sea lions leaving the crate

Patricia Morris is a seal researcher. She works on an island off central California called Año Nuevo. The island is a safe **haven** for thousands of sea lions, seals, and sea birds. It is where many of these animals go when they want to rest, mate, and give birth.

Only a small number of researchers are allowed on the island. They have to move around very carefully to avoid scaring the animals. For this reason, they spend a lot of time working on their hands and knees.

Ten months earlier, on a warm summer morning, Patricia had found a Steller sea lion pup calling for its mother. Patricia could tell that the pup was only a few days old. It was too young to be alone. A sea lion pup spends the first year of its life with its mother. Most likely, waves from a high tide the night before had carried this pup away from its mother.

A sea lion pup calls for its mother.

Two days passed without a sign of the mother sea lion. The pup, which Patricia had named Artemis, was getting weak. Patricia decided to take Artemis to the Marine Mammal Center, a seal hospital on the **mainland**. After receiving permission from a federal agency to move the pup, Patricia crawled out to Artemis. She was careful not to disturb the other sea lion mothers and their pups. Then, she picked up Artemis and crawled back the way she had come.

Artemis spent ten months at the Marine Mammal Center. **Staff** members worked to teach her the skills she would need in the wild. At first, Artemis was fed "fish

A sea lion pup is fed from a bottle.

milkshakes." These are made with ground-up fish, heavy whipping cream, and fish oil. They are high in fat, and they help young pups to gain weight. Artemis drank the milkshakes through a tube, and she quickly put on weight.

The next step was to teach Artemis how to eat fish. Staff members would tie a piece of string around a toy fish and pull it through the water. They wanted Artemis to swim after the fish. Next, staff members put live fish into Artemis's pool to see if she could catch them. After nine months, she had learned to hunt and eat fish on her own.

One day, a **yearling** sea lion named Trent came to the center. Trent was a California sea lion.

California sea lions are smaller than Steller sea lions.

Artemis (bottom) and Trent

Although Artemis was half Trent's age, she was almost double Trent's size. Despite these differences, Artemis and Trent became friends.

A few months later, it was time for the sea lions to be released back into the wild. First, each of the sea lions was fitted with a **transmitter**. The transmitters would track the animals'

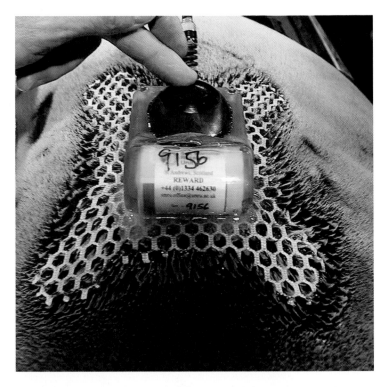

A Steller sea lion is fitted with a transmitter.

Artemis and Trent explore the island.

movements. Artemis's transmitter was glued
to her head and back. The glue did not hurt
Artemis, and the transmitter would fall off
when she lost her hair during her yearly **molt**.

Artemis and Trent spent their first day on
the island together. They explored side by
side. Over the next few days, they separated.
Artemis began to spend more time with
other sea lions.

Artemis (far left) joins other sea lions on the island.

The Marine Mammal Center was pleased to see that Artemis was **adjusting** to life in the wild. Information from the transmitters showed that she was taking deeper dives than she had before. Some of the workers from the center spotted her out in the water when they were boating. They reported that she looked healthy.

The last time Patricia saw Artemis, she noticed that her transmitter was loose. So she wasn't surprised when, a short while later, she no longer received signals from the sea lion. Artemis's transmitter had fallen off into the water. The sea lion pup, now a yearling, had been successfully returned to the wild.

A Steller sea lion dives for food.

CHAPTER THREE

BUGGING OUT

A **swarm** of giant hornets buzzed around Phil DeVries. Some were stinging his hands. Others were spraying poisonous **venom**. Phil was grateful for the special helmet and gloves he was wearing. He knew he might be dead without them.

Phil DeVries is an **entomologist**. He has been fascinated by the insect world since he was three years old. Phil has now traveled the world and studied bugs for more than thirty years.

Giant hornet

Phil DeVries is not afraid to get close to insects in order to study them.

In 2003, *National Geographic* magazine asked Phil to work on a documentary. His assignment was to tour the world with a film crew and find out what makes bugs such incredible survivors.

Phil's first trip was to Tucson, Arizona. Waiting for him there was Justin Schmidt, an entomologist at Southwestern Biological Institute. People call Justin the "King of Sting." Justin invented a system for grading bug stings. He grouped stings into four **categories**. Category-one stings are the least serious stings. Category-four stings can kill.

Justin Schmidt, the King of Sting

Phil volunteered to test the categories. First, he was stung by a bark scorpion. The category-one sting felt hot.

Bark scorpion

Next, he was stung by a red harvester ant. This was a category-three sting, and it hurt quite a bit. Phil did not volunteer to test a category-four sting.

Phil and Justin talked about why some bugs sting. They agreed that stinging bugs are good at defending themselves against bigger animals. These bugs use their stings in order to survive.

Other bugs survive because they are **adaptable**. Phil was about to discover this at

Red harvester ants

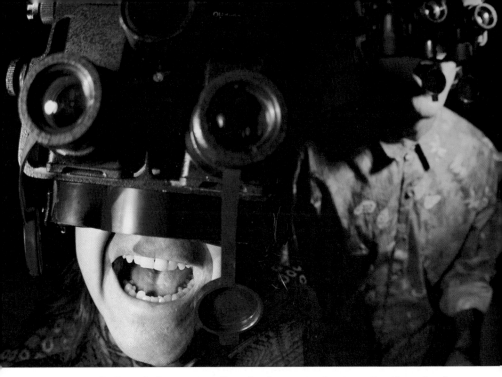

Night-vision goggles help people see in the dark.

his next stop in New York City. There he met with pest-control expert Ed Defreitas. Ed led Phil into an underground tunnel to hunt for cockroaches. Ed knew there would be plenty of roaches in a tunnel because roaches prefer dark, damp places.

Phil and Ed each wore night-vision goggles. The goggles let them see inside the dark tunnel. Because roaches are **sensitive** to sound, the two men sat quietly on the ground. Slowly, roaches began to appear. They clung to the

Cockroach

ceilings. They scuttled across the floor.

Ed explained why roaches survive as well as they do. They have a special type of **bacteria** (bak-TIHR-ee-uh) in their stomachs. The bacteria help them **digest** almost any type of food. This means that roaches can eat just about anything.

Next, Phil tracked down the bot fly in Brazil, a country in South America. Bot flies look like houseflies, but they behave quite differently. Bot fly **larvae** (LARH-vee) can stay alive for weeks by eating living flesh. Even Phil had to admit that he found bot flies disgusting.

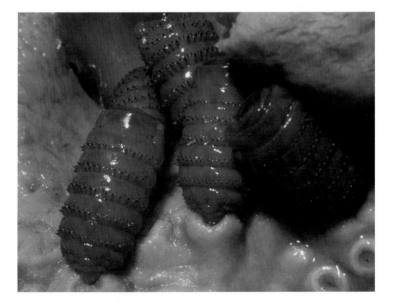

Bot fly larvae eating the flesh in a horse's stomach

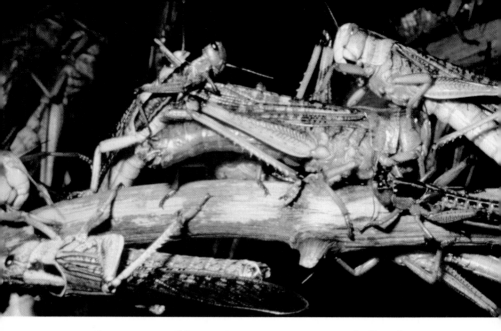

A swarm of locusts can eat as much food as a thousand people can eat at one time.

From Brazil, Phil and his team flew to England to meet with **locust** experts at Oxford University. When locusts swarm, or fly in large groups, they eat any plants in their path. What causes them to swarm?

The experts told Phil that locusts have special hairs on their legs. When the legs are touched, locusts think they are being

By itself, one locust does not cause much damage.

crowded. Quickly, their behavior will
change. Even their shapes and colors will
change. Locusts will then prepare to swarm
in order to move to areas where there are
fewer locusts. Along the way, they eat up
food crops.

Phil's last stop was Tokyo, Japan. There
he met with Masato Ono, an expert on the
giant hornet. Masato has been stung by
giant hornets. He compares the feeling to
"a hot nail being driven into his skin."

Phil and Masato packed a venom
antidote before going on their hunt for
giant hornets. If they were stung, they would
give themselves **injections** to prevent shock.

The men also wore special helmets, or head covers, to protect their heads and faces.

Soon they had found a nest with more than 200 giant hornets. Two giant-hornet guards protected the nest. The guards made noises to alert the others to a disturbance. When the other hornets came out, they sprayed venom at Phil and Masato. The hornets were protecting their queen and her babies inside the nest.

Their work finished, Phil and his crew packed their bags. It had been three months of traveling and filming. Phil hoped the documentary might help people better understand what amazing survivors bugs can be.

Many people learned about insects by watching
Phil's documentary.

CHAPTER FOUR

CALLING ALL REPTILES

Tracey Brown was walking in the desert. With each step she took, a beeping sound could be heard. The beeping came from the receiver Tracey held. It meant that a snake was nearby. Tracey took another step. The receiver beeped louder. A snake must be very close!

Tracey Brown is an **ecologist** who studies reptiles. She spends most of her time looking for lizards and snakes. Sometimes she looks for them in bushes. Other times, she finds them hiding under rocks. She knows that the reptiles she hunts can be anywhere.

Tracey Brown

Tracey Brown (inset) is holding a receiver. She uses
it to track reptiles in the California desert. **37**

Tracking reptiles is a difficult job, especially because most reptiles don't want to be found. Tracey has a good reason for searching them out, though. She wants to track their movements. By tracking reptiles, she hopes to help them survive.

Tracey lives in San Diego, California. San Diego is a large city. More and more people move there all the time. This worries Tracey. Every new house that is built means less land for reptiles.

Thirteen years ago, Tracey decided to help protect reptiles and their land. In her work, Tracey tracks reptiles and finds out where they spend their time. Then she shows her results to area planners. Area planners are responsible for land management. Tracey hopes that if area planners see that certain areas of land are being used by reptiles, they won't allow new development to take place.

Tracey focuses mostly on red diamond rattlesnakes, rosy boas, and horned lizards. Using special equipment, Tracey checks in on the animals she is studying to see where they are and where they have been. This way she knows how much space they need to survive.

After catching a lizard, Tracey takes its measurements. Then she places a tiny backpack on the lizard. Each backpack holds a

Red diamond rattlesnake

Rosy boa

Horned lizard

39

This horned lizard wears a backpack that holds a radio transmitter.

radio transmitter. The radio transmitter sends signals to an **antenna** that Tracey carries. The signals help her track the lizards.

Tracey works differently with snakes. Because they don't have limbs and their backs are rounded, they can't wear backpacks. Instead, Tracey takes the snakes to a hospital. There, a veterinarian cuts a small slit into each snake and puts a transmitter chip inside. Then, the skin is sewed back up.

The chips that are **implanted** into the snakes are very light. Each weighs less than two percent of the snake's weight. After the surgery, the snake must remain at the hospital to heal. After a week, it is set free.

Like the backpacks, the chips respond to Tracey's antenna. They have helped Tracey learn a lot about the snakes' behavior. For instance, she has learned that male snakes travel much greater distances than female snakes in the springtime. Tracey believes they are hunting for mating partners.

Tracey has also learned that most reptiles are more afraid of us than we are of them.

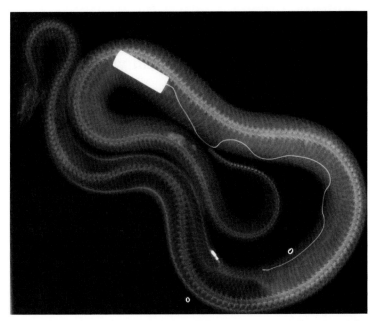

This X ray shows a transmitter chip inside a snake.

Without the radio transmitters, it would be very difficult to find snakes. That's because they blend in with their environment. Without her receiver, Tracey's job would be nearly impossible.

Once, Tracey tracked a female horned lizard for more than a year. One day, the lizard's transmitter no longer responded to Tracey's antenna. Tracey and her team searched everywhere for the lizard. They knew where she liked to spend her time, and they checked all of her favorite spots. Still, the lizard was nowhere to be found.

Five weeks passed, and Tracey worried about the missing lizard. One morning, she drove her car to the study site. Waiting for Tracey was the lost lizard, still wearing her backpack.

Is it possible that the lizard wanted to return to the project? Could it be that the reptiles know she has their best interest at heart? If so, they are right. If Tracey has her way, her research will convince people to slow down land development in San Diego and to leave the reptiles' homes alone.

New construction takes away land from reptiles.

GLOSSARY

adaptable able to change successfully

adjust to get used to a new situation

antenna a metal device used to send and receive signals

antidote a remedy that stops the effects of a poison

audible loud enough to be heard

bacteria (bak-TIHR-ee-uh) one-celled animals that can be seen only with a microscope

category a class of similar things grouped together

communicate to exchange information with another

digest to break down food into energy

documentary a film or program about real people, animals, or events

ecologist a person who studies animals or plants and the places they live

entomologist a person who studies insects

haven a safe place

implant to place an organ or a device inside the body by surgery

injection a shot of medicine given with a needle

larvae (LARH-vee) the young of certain insects after hatching, such as caterpillars

locust a flying insect that eats and destroys crops

mainland a large area of land near an island

molt to shed an outer covering, such as hair or feathers, so that a new one may grow

poacher a person who illegally hunts animals protected by law

sensitive able to see or feel small differences

staff a group of people who work for the same company or organization

swarm a large group of flying insects; to fly in large groups

transmitter a device that sends out radio signals

venom a poison given by one animal to another through a bite or sting

yearling an animal that is one year old

FIND OUT MORE

Eavesdropping on Elephants
www.birds.cornell.edu/brp/EleLP.html
Listen in on the sounds made by forest elephants in Africa.

Saving Artemis
www.tmmc.org
Read more about the rescue of sea lions at the Marine
Mammal Center's Web site.

Bugging Out
www.insects.org
See hundreds of photos of the many kinds of insects that
share our planet.

Calling All Reptiles
www.sandiegozoo.org/animalbytes/t-rattlesnake.html
Learn cool facts about rattlesnakes and other reptiles at this
Web site run by the San Diego Zoo.

More Books to Read

The Bug Scientists by Donna M. Jackson, Houghton
Mifflin Company, 2004

Reptile Rescue by Peggy Thomas, Millbrook Press, 2000

San Francisco's Famous Sea Lions by Kat Shehata, Angel Bea
Publishing, 2003

*Secrets of Sound: Studying the Calls of Whales, Elephants,
and Birds* by April Pulley Sayre, Houghton Mifflin
Company, 2002

INDEX

PHOTO CREDITS

MEET THE AUTHOR

Kirsten Hall began writing books for children when she was thirteen years old, and now has over sixty titles in print. Most of her stories are written for children who are just learning to read. She especially loves to write in rhyme.

After graduating from college in 1996, Hall taught for several years. She worked with preschoolers, kindergartners, and second graders. Now she works as a children's book editor in her hometown, New York City.

Hall has always loved animals. As a child, she spent many summers attending the Bronx Zoo Day Camp where she learned about animals from all over the world.